JAMESTOWN EDUCATION

In the Spotlight™

Volume 1

Levels B–D

Henry Billings

Melissa Billings

 Glencoe

New York, New York   Columbus, Ohio   Chicago, Illinois   Peoria, Illinois   Woodland Hills, California

JAMESTOWN EDUCATION

Glencoe

The *McGraw·Hill* Companies

ISBN-13: 978-0-07-874318-4
ISBN-10: 0-07-874318-4

Send all queries to:
Glencoe/McGraw-Hill
8787 Orion Place
Columbus, OH 43240-4027

2 3 4 5 6 7 8 9 10 021 10 09 08 07

Contents

Unit Three

To the Student

This book has nine articles about celebrities, or famous people, in the world today. Some of the celebrities are movie or television stars. Some are sports players. Others are authors or musicians.

The lives of these stars can inspire us. Some of the stars had tough times while growing up. They worked very hard to find success. Others had to stay focused on their dreams even when other people thought they would fail. And some had to get through challenges even after they became well-known.

In this book you will work on these three specific reading skills:

Main Idea and Supporting Details

Sequence

Author's Purpose

You will also work on other reading and vocabulary skills. This will help you understand and think about what you read. The lessons include types of questions often found on state and national tests. Completing the questions can help you get ready for tests you may have to take later.

How to Use This Book

About the Book

This book has three units. Each unit has three lessons. Each lesson has an article about a celebrity followed by practice exercises.

Working Through Each Lesson

Photo Start each lesson by looking at the photo. Read the title and subtitle to get an idea of what the article will focus on.

Think About What You Know, Word Power, Reading Skill This page will help you prepare to read.

Article Now read about the celebrity. Enjoy!

Activities Complete all the activities. Then check your work. Your teacher will give you an answer key to do this. Record the number of your correct answers for each activity. At the end of the lesson, add up your total score for parts A, B, and C. Then find your percentage score in the table. Record your percentage score on the Comprehension and Critical Thinking Progress Graph on page 105.

Compare and Contrast Chart At the end of each unit, you will complete a Compare and Contrast Chart. The chart will help you see what some of the celebrities in the unit have in common.

My Personal Dictionary In the back of this book, you can jot down words you would like to know more about. Later you can ask your teacher or a classmate what the words mean. Then you can add the definitions in your own words.

Will Smith

Thalía

Tony Hawk

Will Smith

Hardest-Working Man in Hollywood

Birth Name Willard Christopher Smith Jr.

Birth Date and Place September 25, 1968; Philadelphia, Pennsylvania

Home a ranch near Malibu, California

Think About What You Know

Have you ever had to work very hard to get something that you wanted? What happened? How did it make you feel? Read the article to find out how hard Will Smith works.

Word Power

What do the words below tell you about the article?

strict keeping tight control

intelligent able to think and learn

career the type of work someone chooses to do

confident sure of one's self

canopy a tentlike covering that blocks the sun

Reading Skill

Main Idea and Supporting Details The most important idea in a paragraph is the **main idea.** Each sentence in the paragraph will be about the main idea. These sentences are called **supporting details.** In some paragraphs, the writer states the main idea in one sentence.

Example	
Main Idea	Last night I went to see a movie. I went with a friend.
Supporting Details	We decided to see a funny movie. We bought a bag of popcorn to share. The movie made us laugh out loud.

"Last night I went to see a movie" is the main idea. Can you give two reasons why this is the main idea?

Will Smith

Hardest-Working Man in Hollywood

He's smart. He's funny. And he's charming. But these are not the only reasons why Will Smith is a star. The truth is that Smith is one of the hardest workers in Hollywood.

2 Will Smith grew up in Philadelphia. He has two sisters and one brother. Smith's father was very **strict**. He made sure his children followed the rules. He would not let them be messy or lazy. Even their sock drawers had to be neat.

3 Smith's father expected his children to do well in school. That was not a problem for Will. As a boy, he loved science. He dreamed of becoming a scientist. "From the age of about 10 to 15, that's all I wanted to be," he says.

4 But Smith was good at lots of other things as well. When he was 12, he began to fool around with music. He turned out to be a pretty good rapper. By age 16, he was calling himself the Fresh Prince.

5 Smith worked with another young rapper, DJ Jazzy Jeff. At first Smith used foul language like other rappers. But then his grandmother found his music book. She read it and wrote a note in the back. He remembers that the note said:

6 "Dear Willard,

7 "Truly **intelligent** people do not have to use these types of words to express themselves."

8 That was all it took. Smith did not want to hurt his grandmother's feelings. He knew how much she loved him. As he says, she "believed I could do anything." From then on, he wrote different music. It was still rap. But it had clean language. People loved it.

9   In 1985, when Smith was 17, he had to make a hard choice. A record company gave him and Jazzy Jeff a chance to record their music. On the one hand, he wanted a **career** in music. But on the other hand, he wanted to go to college. He had been planning to go to MIT. That's one of the best colleges in the country. Smith could keep making music. Or he could go to MIT and study computers. Will's parents told him it was his choice. They would stand behind him no matter what he did.

10   In the end, Smith chose music. By the time he was 21, he had won his first Grammy Award. He had also won the hearts of many people in Hollywood. Smith was friendly to everyone. He was always smiling. And there was something else. He believed in himself. He was so **confident** that he made others believe too.

11   Smith had never been an actor. He had never taken a single acting class. But he put out the word that he would like to be on TV. Soon he had his own TV show (*The Fresh Prince of Bel-Air*).

12   Next Smith began making movies. He starred in such hits as *Independence Day* (1996) and *Men in Black* (1997). For his role in *Ali* (2001), he came close to winning an Academy Award. Smith became one of the highest-paid actors in the world. For *I, Robot* (2004), he made $28 million.

Skill Break
Main Idea and Supporting Details

Look at paragraph 9 on this page. The paragraph gives **details** about two things Will Smith wanted to do. He wanted to go to college. But he also wanted to make music. These details support the **main idea.**

What is the **main idea** of the paragraph?

13 Smith knows he is lucky. He is the first to admit it. But he also knows that people often make their own luck. They do it through hard work.

14 "Whoever puts in the most time and works the hardest and wants it the most is going to win," he says. "It just doesn't work out any other way." Smith believes that is how he stands out from other actors or rappers. As he puts it, "Nobody is going to work as hard as me." He adds, "When I was growing up, there were rappers who could rap way better than me, but while they were sleeping, I was rapping. While they were eating, I was rapping. While they were out chasing girls, I was rapping."

15 Smith isn't kidding about working hard. One example came when he was making *Independence Day*. The crew was filming in the Utah desert. It was 120 degrees. A **canopy** was set up to give people some shade. Says one man, "Everyone was under the canopy except Will. He was still out there being his own stand-in. That set the tone for the rest of the movie. Will led by example."

16 Of course, Smith has had some hard times too. His first marriage did not work out. But in 1997, he married Jada Pinkett. This marriage has lasted. He and Jada have a son and a daughter. They also spend a lot of time with Smith's son from his first marriage.

Fun Facts

▶ Smith likes to play chess and golf.

▶ He has a brother and a sister who are twins.

▶ He turned down the role of Neo in *The Matrix* (1999).

Will Smith has won a number of Grammy Awards for his rap music.

17   Will Smith has already had a great career. He's been a top rapper. He's been a star on TV and in the movies. Who knows what might come next? The man seems able to do almost anything. He has even joked about becoming the president of the United States. But whatever he does, he will work hard at it. Says Smith, "If you're not willing to work hard, let someone else do it. I'd rather be with someone who does a horrible job but gives 110 percent than with someone who does a good job and gives 60 percent."

◆ Fill in the circle next to the correct answer.

1. As a boy, Smith dreamed about being

○ A. a scientist.

○ B. a rapper.

○ C. the president.

2. Smith stopped using bad language in his rap music because

○ A. his father found his music and got angry.

○ B. Jazzy Jeff wanted him to write clean songs.

○ C. he did not want to hurt his grandmother's feelings.

3. What was the effect of Smith's getting to record his music with a record company?

○ A. He started calling himself the Fresh Prince.

○ B. He changed his mind about going to college.

○ C. He decided to start making movies.

4. From the information in the article, you can predict that Smith will

○ A. star in another TV show.

○ B. want to become a sports star.

○ C. keep on making hit movies.

5. What lesson about life does this story teach?

○ A. Working hard can help you get ahead.

○ B. Safety is always the most important thing.

○ C. Everyone has a bad day once in a while.

_____ Number of Correct Answers: Part A

B Finding the Main Idea and Supporting Details

◆ Read each paragraph below. Fill in the circle next to the sentence that **best** states the main idea of the paragraph.

1.

Smith isn't kidding about working hard. One example came when he was making *Independence Day*. The crew was filming in the Utah desert. It was 120 degrees. A canopy was set up to give people some shade. Says one man, "Everyone was under the canopy except Will. He was still out there being his own stand-in. That set the tone for the rest of the movie. Will led by example."

○ A. The crew was filming in the Utah desert.
○ B. A canopy was set up to give people some shade.
○ C. Will led by example.

2.

In the end, Smith chose music. By the time he was 21, he had won his first Grammy Award. He had also won the hearts of many people in Hollywood. Smith was friendly to everyone. He was always smiling. And there was something else. He believed in himself. He was so confident that he made others believe too.

○ A. By the time he was 21, Smith had won his first Grammy Award.
○ B. He was always smiling.
○ C. He believed in himself.

_____ Number of Correct Answers: Part B

C Using Words

◆ Complete each sentence with a word from the box. Write the missing word on the line.

strict	**career**	**canopy**
intelligent	**confident**	

1. The girls felt hot in the sun so they set up a _____.

2. My teacher is very _____ about making me raise my hand in class.

3. Choosing a job that is right for you could lead to a great

_____.

4. The runner smiled because he felt _____ that he would win the race.

5. The _____ teacher found the answer quickly.

◆ Choose one word from the box. Write a new sentence using the word.

6. word: _____

_____

_____ Number of Correct Answers: Part C

D Writing About It

Write a Postcard

◆ Write a postcard to Will Smith. Finish the sentences below to write your postcard. Use the checklist on page 103 to check your work.

Dear Mr. Smith,
    I just read an article about you. I think

you _____ .

I was glad to hear that_____

_____ .

I hope that you will _____

_____ .

                 Sincerely,

              _____

Mr. Will Smith
123 Smith Ave.
Willstown, USA

Lesson 1 Add your correct answers from parts A, B, and C to get your total score. Then find the percentage for your total score on the chart below. Record your percentage on the graph on page 105.

_____ Total Score for Parts A, B, and C

_____ Percentage

Total Score	1	2	3	4	5	6	7	8	9	10	11	12	13
Percentage	8	15	23	31	38	46	54	62	69	77	85	92	100

Thalía

From the Dark into the Light

Birth Name Ariadna Thalía Sodi Miranda

Birth Date and Place August 26, 1972; Mexico City, Mexico

Homes New York City and Miami, Florida

Think About What You Know

Have you ever felt very sad, very afraid, or very tired? How did you get through those hard times? Read the article to find out how Thalía learned to be strong during hard times.

Word Power

What do the words below tell you about the article?

local within the same town

producer a person in charge of making a work of art

disaster a terrible event

desperate having little or no hope

gallery a place where art is sold

Reading Skill

Sequence The order of ideas in an article is called **sequence.** A good sequence clearly shows the order in which things happen. The author often uses words such as *first, next, then,* and *finally* to show the order.

Example	
Happens first	First, Sam took a music class at school. Then
Happens second	he joined a band.

"Sam took a music class" is the first thing that happened. "He joined a band" is the second thing that happened. What words show that Sam joined the band after he took the class? What other words can you think of that might show sequence?

Thalía

From the Dark into the Light

In some ways, Thalía Sodi's life has been a fairy tale. But it has also been a nightmare. She began performing at age nine. By age 13, she was a star. She has millions of fans around the world. But she has also had more than her share of troubles. Still, this Mexican superstar always finds her way back to happiness. As she puts it, she has learned to turn "darkness into light."

2   Thalía was born in Mexico in 1972. She was the youngest of five daughters. Thalía loved her father with all her heart. But when she was just five years old, he died. She was crushed. "I didn't talk for one whole year," she recalls.

3   After that, Thalía's mother took her aside. She told Thalía to be strong. Thalía knew her mother was right. She had to be strong and get on with her life. With her mother's help, she did just that.

4   By the time Thalía was eight, her oldest sister Laura was already grown up. Laura was an actress in a **local** theater. Thalía loved to watch her perform. She recalls, "I had to behave in school the whole week to go see her play in the theater. Every time I saw her onstage it was like, 'I can't believe she's my sister! She's the same sister I knew, but onstage she's another person. How does she do that?'" That's when Thalía decided that she, too, wanted a career in acting and music.

5   Over the next few years, Thalía set out to make her dream come true. She took ballet classes. She took piano lessons. She joined a children's singing group. Soon she became the lead singer in a band called Timbiriche. She also won a role on a Mexican TV soap opera.

6   In the late 1980's, Thalía's singing career began to go very well. First she spent a year in California. Then, in 1989, her first album

came out. It was called *Thalía*. During this time, Thalía fell in love with a man named Alfredo Diaz Ordaz. He was one of the people who helped her make her recordings. Soon the two of them made plans to get married. But then Alfredo became sick. He had liver cancer. When Alfredo died, Thalía was just 22.

7   Bravely, Thalía went on with her life. She started to work harder. From 1992 to 1995, she starred in three Mexican soap operas. In each one, she played a poor young woman trying to find happiness. These shows were big hits. They made Thalía a bigger star than ever. Everyone in Mexico knew who she was. People from Brazil to Indonesia also watched her TV shows. They, too, fell in love with Thalía.

8   Thalía kept singing. She made new albums. These sold millions of copies. She traveled, taking her music to people around the world. Wherever she went, fans stood in line for hours to see her. But again, trouble was soon to come. In 1998 Thalía collapsed. She was completely worn out. "I couldn't move. I couldn't even open my eyes," she says. She had been "working, working, working nonstop since I was nine years old." It had finally all caught up with her. It took her almost a year to get her strength back.

9   After some time, Thalía was ready to work again. She made a movie, *Mambo Café* (2000). She fell in love and married record **producer** Tommy Mottola. Then, in 2001, she was considered for a Latin Grammy Award.

Skill Break
Sequence
Look at paragraph 9 on this page. The paragraph tells more about Thalía's life.

What happened *after* Thalía married Tommy Mottola?

10   At last it looked as though things were going well for her. But again, **disaster** struck. It happened early one Sunday morning in September 2002. Two of Thalía's sisters, Laura and Ernestina, were driving home from an evening at the theater. Suddenly a group of men attacked their car. The two women were kidnapped. They were not hurt, but the men demanded $1 million to set them free.

11   Thalía was **desperate** to help her sisters. She was very close to both of them. The Sodi family did not want the police involved. They did not want to give the kidnappers any reason to kill Laura and Ernestina. Friends say that Thalía talked with the kidnappers on the phone several times. They say she helped put together the $1 million the kidnappers wanted. Thalía herself does not like to talk about it. But clearly this was a very hard time for her.

12   Luckily, both sisters were finally set free. "I'm very thankful," Thalía says. "Millions of people prayed for us."

13   After this, some people thought Thalía might be afraid to go out in public. After all, someone could try to kidnap *her*. But Thalía refuses to be afraid. In fact, she feels she owes it to her fans to keep performing. She says, "So many people have opened their hearts for me, now I want to make them dance, be happy, and have a good time." She really means it. She'll do anything to please her fans. In 2003 she traveled through Texas. At one stop, she signed 2,800 autographs!

Fun Facts

▸ Thalía collects dolls and stuffed animals.

▸ She drinks lots of water every day.

▸ She likes skiing and rock climbing.

Thalía believes that her work is to give happiness to her fans.

14   These days Thalía is busier than ever. She has started a line of clothing for a big chain store. She has a line of chocolates. In 2004 Thalía even opened her own art show. She put 18 of her paintings in a New York **gallery.** Some of the money she makes from selling them will be used to help poor children in Mexico.

15   Looking back over her life, Thalía has reason to be proud. She has been through some very hard times. Yet she is stronger now than ever. Maybe that's why, when asked about her future, she says she sees "a lot of happiness."

A Understanding What You Read

◆ **Fill in the circle next to the correct answer.**

1. What was the cause of Thalía's not talking for one whole year?

○ A. She was very tired.

○ B. Her father died.

○ C. Her mother got sick.

2. Thalía wanted a career in acting and music because she

○ A. wanted to be rich and well-known.

○ B. got a part in a Mexican soap opera.

○ C. saw her sister onstage doing plays.

3. In which paragraph did you find the information to answer question 2?

○ A. paragraph 4

○ B. paragraph 5

○ C. paragraph 6

4. What does Thalía do with some of the money she makes from her paintings?

○ A. She spends it on new clothes.

○ B. She gives it to her sisters.

○ C. She uses it to help poor children.

5. Which sentence **best** states the main idea of the article?

○ A. Thalía has fallen in love many times in her life.

○ B. Thalía has never let hard times stop her from moving on.

○ C. Thalía has tried to make smart decisions about her career.

_____ Number of Correct Answers: Part A

B Finding the Sequence

◆ Read the paragraph below. It shows a sequence. Number the sentences below the paragraph to show the order of what happened.

1.

    In the late 1980's, Thalía's singing career began to go very well. First she spent a year in California. Then, in 1989, her first album came out. It was called *Thalía*. During this time, Thalía fell in love with a man named Alfredo Diaz Ordaz. He was one of the people who helped her make her recordings. Soon the two of them made plans to get married. But then Alfredo became sick. He had liver cancer. When Alfredo died, Thalía was just 22.

_____ Alfredo became sick and died.

_____ Thalía and Alfredo planned to marry.

_____ Thalía spent a year in California.

_____ Thalía's first album came out.

◆ Which words helped show you the sequence? Circle the sequence words in the paragraph. Then write the words on the lines below.

2. _____

    _____

    _____

_____ Number of Correct Answers: Part B

C Using Words

Complete each sentence with a word from the box. Write the missing word on the line.

local	disaster	gallery
producer	desperate	

1. The fire in the barn was a terrible _____.

2. The singer thanked the _____ for helping her make a great record.

3. They went to the _____ shoe store because they did not want to drive far.

4. She went to see the paintings in the _____.

5. After he ran out of water, he was _____ for something to drink.

Choose a word from the box. Write a new sentence using the word.

6. word: _____

_____

D Writing About It

Write a Speech

◆ Write a speech about Thalía and how she helps others. Finish
the sentences below to write your speech. Use the checklist on
page 103 to check your work.

Thalía is not only a great singer but also a very giving person.

For example, Thalía once helped her family by _____

_____.

She also gives to people outside her own family. Thalía gives to her

fans by _____

_____.

Thalía also helps poor people by _____

_____.

Lesson 2 Add your correct answers from parts A, B, and C to get your total
score. Then find the percentage for your total score on the chart below.
Record your percentage on the graph on page 105.

_____ Total Score for Parts A, B, and C

_____ Percentage

Total Score	1	2	3	4	5	6	7	8	9	10	11	12	13
Percentage	8	15	23	31	38	46	54	62	69	77	85	92	100

Tony Hawk

Doing Things His Way

Birth Name Anthony Frank Hawk

Birth Date and Place May 12, 1968; San Diego, California

Home Carlsbad, California

Think About What You Know

Have you ever practiced a lot so that you could do something new? How much practice did it take? Read the article to find out how Tony Hawk did something no one had ever done before.

Word Power

What do the words below tell you about the article?

drills practice that is the same each time

skinny very thin

companies groups of people who make or sell something

sprained hurt by bending too far

stretcher a small bed used to carry someone who is hurt

Reading Skill

Author's Purpose When authors write, they write for a reason. This reason is called the **author's purpose.** The author might want to tell about a person, place, or thing. The author might want to get the reader to think a certain way. The author might also want to make the reader laugh and enjoy the story.

Example

One of the first skateboards was made in Florida in 1961. A kid named Bob Schmidt made it. He worked on it with his friends. They made it out of their sisters' roller skates and a piece of wood.

In this paragraph the author's purpose is *to tell about* one of the first skateboards. One clue is that the author gives facts to help the reader learn something. What other clues show that the author's purpose is *to tell about* something?

Tony Hawk
Doing Things His Way

No one had ever done it. Even Tony Hawk hadn't mastered it. But that didn't keep Hawk from dreaming about it. He thought that maybe, someday, he could make it happen. If anyone could do it, Hawk was the one. He came up with new skateboarding tricks all the time. In all, he had made up close to 100 new tricks.

2   This one, though, would be special. Hawk called it the "900." There are 360 degrees in a circle. So two and one half circles equals 900 degrees. Hawk's dream was to flip two and one half times in the air. Hawk would only have two seconds to do these flips. That's how long he could stay in the air before hitting the ground.

3   Hawk worked years getting ready for the 900. He worked on each part of the trick. He practiced the takeoff. He worked on his body position. Hawk did tens of thousands of "360" flips in the air. Still, he wasn't ready for the full 900.

4   "I thought up the trick in 1986," he later said, "but didn't have the guts to try it for 10 years."

5   Even without the 900, Hawk was the world's greatest skateboarder. He had first fallen in love with the sport at the age of nine. At that time, he played basketball and baseball as well. But Hawk didn't like the shooting and throwing **drills.** He didn't like having to follow orders. Skateboarding was not like that at all. With skateboarding, Hawk could do his own thing. He could be free. "It's not someone telling you what to do. That was the bottom line," Hawk said. "I just didn't want to be ordered around."

6   Hawk quickly gave up his other sports. He practiced skateboarding hour after hour, day after day. He didn't mind the work. There was no coach telling him what to do. He could decide for himself when to start and when to stop.

7   Hawk was tall but not strong. That was a problem. A skateboarder needs strength to get the board high in the air. Hawk did not have strong arms. He had trouble lifting his board to do tricks. He later said, "Because I was really **skinny,** I had a hard time." Still, Hawk found a way to work around the problem. He came up with his own style. He learned to leap up into the air with the board still on his feet.

8   As a teenager, Hawk spent a lot of time alone. He didn't fit in with the kids at school. He didn't go to dances or parties. He spent his free time skateboarding. Other kids often laughed at him. They told him that skateboarding was for "losers."

9   "I used to get teased all the time," said Hawk. "People made fun of me."

10   But Hawk had the support of the two people who counted most, his mother and father. His mom said he had been a "difficult" child. But once he found skateboarding, that changed. All his energy went into practicing. His dad even helped to start skateboard clubs in California.

Skill Break
Author's Purpose
So far the author has talked about Tony Hawk and his dream to do a "900." The author has also talked about some of the problems Hawk had as a child.

From what you have read so far, what might the **author's purpose** be in this article?

11   At the age of 12, Hawk won his first contest. Two years later, in 1982, he turned pro. Hawk quickly rose to the top of the skateboarding world. He won almost every contest he entered. He became the biggest name in the sport. In time, he made his own video game. It was called Tony Hawk's Pro Skater. He also started two **companies.** One sold skateboarding clothes. The other made skateboards.

12   Hawk gave names to his skateboarding tricks. One was the Stale Fish. Another was the 720 McHawk. Many of his tricks were amazing. But they were also dangerous. He often got hurt doing them. He **sprained** his ankles and wrists many times. He cracked his ribs. He broke an elbow. He hurt his knee. "My upper front teeth are fake," he told a reporter. "I broke them out three times." Even so, Hawk kept performing. And he kept dreaming of that 900.

13   At last, on June 27, 1999, he felt ready to do it. He would try the 900 at the X Games in San Francisco. There was a special contest called "Best Trick." Eight thousand screaming fans filled the stands. Many more watched on TV. "I was either going to make it or be carried off the ramp on a **stretcher,**" he said.

Fun Facts

▸ Hawk likes to surf and watch movies.

▸ He used to practice skating in empty swimming pools.

▸ He got his first skateboard from his brother.

▸ He gives money to build skateboard parks around the country.

Tony Hawk flies through the air during one of his tricks.

14   On his first try, he fell. He fell on his second try too. He fell on his third and fourth tries. But each time he was getting closer. The other skaters stopped their tricks to watch. They wanted to cheer him on. So they banged their boards on the ramp as he climbed to the top of the "half-pipe." Ten times Hawk tried. Ten times he failed. Twice he almost made it. But the board slipped out from under him.

15   Then, on his eleventh try, he did it. He did two and a half flips. And he made a clean landing. The crowd went wild. The other skaters jumped with joy. Tony Hawk had finally landed a 900.

16   "This is the best day of my life," Hawk told the crowd.

17   Skateboarding fans knew that Tony Hawk's career would not last forever. He was already in his 30s. But as one skateboarder put it, "It will be a long time before anyone like him comes along again."

A Understanding What You Read

◆ **Fill in the circle next to the correct answer.**

1. Why did Hawk give up his other sports?

○ A. His parents didn't like basketball.

○ B. He didn't like having to follow orders.

○ C. He hurt his knee and broke his elbow.

2. Hawk once had a problem doing skateboard tricks because

○ A. he did not have strong arms.

○ B. his skateboard was too heavy.

○ C. he was afraid of getting hurt.

3. Choose the statement below that states an opinion.

○ A. I thought up the trick in 1986.

○ B. My upper front teeth are fake.

○ C. This is the best day of my life.

4. From what you read in the article, which of these is probably true?

○ A. People all over the world love skateboarding.

○ B. Few people will be able to copy the "900."

○ C. Tony Hawk's video game is hard to play.

5. Which of the following groups would this article fit into?

○ A. Dreams That Came True

○ B. Best Places to Visit

○ C. Things That People Made

_____ Number of Correct Answers: Part A

B Finding the Author's Purpose

◆ What is the author's purpose for writing the article about Tony Hawk? Fill in the circle next to the phrase that **best** states the author's purpose.

1.

- ○ A. to get the reader to want to try skateboarding
- ○ B. to make the reader laugh about a funny skateboarding story
- ○ C. to tell the reader about a famous skateboarder

◆ Read the short article below. What is the author's purpose for writing the article? Fill in the circle next to the phrase that **best** states the author's purpose.

2.

People once thought skateboarding was just for boys. Today, that's hard to believe. Girls' skateboarding is growing quickly. Many top skaters are women. It's about time!

We have come a long way. And it keeps getting better. Girls do not have to feel shy about skateboarding. Now they even have all-girl skateboard camps. And girls have great women skaters to look up to.

- ○ A. to get the reader to like the idea of girls' skateboarding
- ○ B. to make the reader laugh about girls' skateboarding
- ○ C. to tell the reader how women's skateboarding started

_____ Number of Correct Answers: Part B

C Using Words

◆ Complete each sentence with a word from the box. Write the missing word on the line.

drills	companies	stretcher
skinny	sprained	

1. He tripped over the cat and _____ his ankle.

2. The man who broke his leg was carried on a

_____.

3. Our dog is very _____, so we give him extra food.

4. We have fire _____ at school.

5. Both _____ make the same kind of clothes.

◆ Choose one word from the box. Write a new sentence using the word.

6. word: _____

_____

_____

_____ Number of Correct Answers: Part C

D Writing About It

Write a News Article

◆ Suppose you were a reporter at the 1999 X Games. Write a news article about Tony Hawk's 900. Finish the sentences below to write your news article. Use the checklist on page 103 to check your work.

Fans cheered wildly at the X Games when Tony Hawk _____

_____ .

The 900 is a _____

_____ .

When he landed, the other skaters _____

_____ .

Hawk told the crowd, "This is the best day of my life."

Lesson 3 Add your correct answers from parts A, B, and C to get your total score. Then find the percentage for your total score on the chart below. Record your percentage on the graph on page 105.

_____ Total Score for Parts A, B, and C

_____ Percentage

Total Score	1	2	3	4	5	6	7	8	9	10	11	12	13
Percentage	8	15	23	31	38	46	54	62	69	77	85	92	100

Compare and Contrast

◆ Think about the celebrities, or famous people, in Unit One. Pick two articles that tell about celebrities who had help from their families. Use information from the articles to fill in this chart.

Celebrity's Name		
Who helped from the celebrity's family?		
What did the family do to help?		
How did this help change the celebrity's life?		

Tobey Maguire

Grant Hill

J. K. Rowling

Tobey Maguire
From Cook to Superhero

Birth Name Tobias Vincent Maguire
Birth Date and Place June 27, 1975; Santa Monica, California
Home Los Angeles, California

Think About What You Know

Do you know someone who likes to act? Have you ever wondered how big movie stars get started in acting? Read the article to find out how Tobey Maguire got his start.

Word Power

What do the words below tell you about the article?

audition to try out for a part in a play or movie

communicating sharing ideas and feelings

physical having to do with the body

jockey a person who rides a race horse

stunts dangerous actions

Reading Skill

Main Idea and Supporting Details The most important idea in a paragraph is the **main idea.** Each sentence in the paragraph will be about the main idea. These sentences are called **supporting details.** In some paragraphs, the writer states the main idea in one sentence.

Example	
Main Idea	Everyone in my family likes comic books. My
Supporting Details	brother reads comic books. My sister reads comic books. Even my parents read comic books.

"Everyone in my family likes comic books" is the main idea. Can you give two reasons why this is the main idea?

Tobey Maguire

From Cook to Superhero

His father worked as a cook, and his grandmother taught cooking. So it was not surprising that Tobey Maguire loved being in a kitchen. When he was in junior high school, Maguire signed up to take a cooking class.

2 His mother, however, didn't want him to do that. She wanted him to take an acting class instead. She offered him $100 to change classes. To Maguire, that was a lot of money. So he took the cash and switched classes. As a result, the world may have lost a cook, but it gained a fine actor.

3 From the start, it was clear that Maguire had talent. He had a way of acting without seeming to act. While still in junior high school, he made several TV commercials. He quickly moved on to small parts in TV shows such as *Roseanne*. At age 17, he landed his first big part. He was picked for the starring role on a show called *Great Scott!* It aired on network TV in 1992. Maguire was good, very good. But the show did not get good ratings and ended after just six weeks.

Skill Break

Main Idea and Supporting Details

Look at paragraph 3 on this page. The paragraph gives **details** about Tobey Maguire. He could act without seeming to act. He got jobs on TV. And at age 17 he starred in the show *Great Scott!* These details support the **main idea.**

What is the **main idea** of the paragraph?

4   The following year, Maguire crossed over to movies. He won a small role in *This Boy's Life*. The film was a hit, and Maguire's future looked bright. But then Maguire appeared in several other movies. None did well, and all were quickly forgotten. That raised a troubling question. Was Tobey Maguire really that good an actor? Even Maguire himself began to have doubts.

5   Things got worse in 1995. A man named Allan Moyle was making a movie called *Empire Records*. He wanted Maguire to star in it. First, of course, Maguire had to **audition** for the part. That turned out to be a problem. "When I went in to read for the film I wasn't prepared," says Maguire. "I disappointed Allan, and I disappointed myself."

6   Maguire ended up with only a small part. Even that proved too much for him. Before the movie was finished, Maguire asked to be dropped from the cast. "I was just having a rough time **communicating** with people," he says. "I think I had a lot of anger . . . I just needed to get some things in order."

7   Maguire took a break from acting. After a few months, he felt much better. He returned to Hollywood more determined than ever to do well. This time things went much better. He earned great reviews for his role in *The Ice Storm* (1997). He went on to win praise for his work in *Pleasantville* (1998), *The Cider House Rules* (1999), and *Wonder Boys* (2000).

8   Then, in 2002, Maguire went from star to superstar. He did it by taking on the role of Peter Parker in *Spider-Man*. This character starts out as a regular kid with the usual problems. But one day a strange spider bites him, giving him special powers. Suddenly he can climb walls like a spider. Soon Peter Parker becomes Spider-Man!

9   Until this movie, Maguire had gone after serious roles in serious films. Now he was playing a comic book superhero. Why did he take this part? There was something about Spider-Man that Maguire liked. After all, "Spidey" is not your average superhero. He doesn't come from outer space like Superman. He doesn't have tons of money like Batman. As one man says, "He's a kid who goes to school. He's slightly unpopular. He's got money problems." And he loses his uncle, who is like a father to him.

10   "He's one of us," Maguire agrees. "We can imagine ourselves in his position."

11   The role of Spider-Man offered plenty of **physical** challenges. Maguire wasn't big or packed with muscles. So he had to build himself up. "I worked out for five months," he says. He exercised six days a week. He ran, biked, and lifted weights. Only then was he ready to wear Spider-Man's blue and red suit.

12   The suit was a challenge all by itself. It had to be skintight. Workers made more than 30 suits. Finally they came up with one that was snug enough. "Sometimes they would have to sew me into the suit because the zippers would break all the time," says Maguire.

13   To create the suit, the workers made a special cast of Maguire's body. When the cast dried on his skin, it stuck to the hair on his arms and legs. Taking it off was not fun. "It ripped probably two thirds of the hair out of my legs," says Maguire. "I can still feel it."

Fun Facts

- Maguire likes to do yoga and play basketball.
- He does not eat meat.
- He has a fear of heights.
- Robert DeNiro is one of his favorite actors.

The *Spider-Man* movies made Tobey Maguire a big star.

14   *Spider-Man* was a huge hit. And from there, Maguire moved on to *Seabiscuit* (2003). In this movie Maguire plays a half-blind **jockey.** Again, the role was physically tough. Maguire had to lose 20 pounds. But he also had to be strong enough to handle a race horse. He was surprised at how much leg strength was needed. "I couldn't believe that after a couple of minutes my legs were like noodles," he said. "I could barely stand up."

15   *Seabiscuit* was another winner. And then came *Spider-Man 2* (2004). Once again, Maguire had to build up his body weight. He also had to climb back into that suit! *Spider-Man 2* had even more **stunts.** And the stunts were more difficult. Still, Maguire was up to the challenge. Many people said *Spider-Man 2* was even better than the first *Spider-Man*.

16   Today Maguire is one of the biggest stars in Hollywood. Although he is still young, his life has already had lots of interesting twists and turns. The biggest, perhaps, came back in junior high school, with his mother's offer of $100 to switch classes.

A ▪ Understanding What You Read

◆ Fill in the circle next to the correct answer.

1. Tobey Maguire's mother wanted him to

    ○ A. learn to ride a horse.

    ○ B. take an acting class.

    ○ C. become a good cook.

2. Why did Maguire like the idea of playing Spider-Man?

    ○ A. He felt Spider-Man was a lot like a real person.

    ○ B. He wanted to do more dangerous stunts.

    ○ C. He liked the idea of being in a serious film.

3. From what you read in the article, *Spider-Man* and *Spider-Man 2* are different because

    ○ A. Maguire did not act in *Spider-Man 2*.

    ○ B. there were fewer surprises in *Spider-Man 2*.

    ○ C. the stunts in *Spider-Man 2* were harder.

4. If you were a parent, how might you use the information in this article to help your children?

    ○ A. I would encourage them to try new things.

    ○ B. I would pay them to go to school.

    ○ C. I would cook them good-tasting food.

5. The author probably wrote this article in order to

    ○ A. make readers laugh about Maguire's cooking class.

    ○ B. tell readers about Maguire's acting career.

    ○ C. get readers to go see Maguire in *Spider-Man*.

_____ Number of Correct Answers: Part A

B Finding the Main Idea and Supporting Details

◆ Read each paragraph below. Fill in the circle next to the sentence that **best** states the main idea of the paragraph.

1.

Things got worse in 1995. A man named Allan Moyle was making a movie called *Empire Records*. He wanted Maguire to star in it. First, of course, Maguire had to audition for the part. That turned out to be a problem. "When I went in to read for the film I wasn't prepared," says Maguire. "I disappointed Allan, and I disappointed myself."

○ A. Maguire had to audition for the part.
○ B. He wanted Maguire to star in it.
○ C. Things got worse in 1995.

2.

The suit was a challenge all by itself. It had to be skintight. Workers made more than 30 suits. Finally they came up with one that was snug enough. "Sometimes they would have to sew me into the suit because the zippers would break all the time," says Maguire.

○ A. The suit was a challenge all by itself.
○ B. It had to be skintight.
○ C. Workers made more than 30 suits.

_____ Number of Correct Answers: Part B

C Using Words

◆ Complete each sentence with a word from the box. Write the missing word on the line.

audition	physical	stunts
communicating	jockey	

1. The speech teacher was good at _____ with

her class.

2. The singer had to _____ for a part in the show.

3. He wore a helmet when he was doing _____.

4. He became a _____ because he loved horses.

5. Riding a bike is more _____ than riding in a car.

◆ Choose one word from the box. Write a new sentence using the word.

6. word: _____

_____

_____

_____ Number of Correct Answers: Part C

D Writing About It

Write Your Thoughts

◆ Answer the question below. Use the checklist on page 103 to check your work.

Would you recommend this article to other students? Explain.

_____

_____

_____

How Did You Do?

◆ Finish the sentences below. Use the checklist on page 103 to check your work.

One of the things I did best when reading this article was _____

_____.

I believe I did this well because _____

_____.

Lesson 4 Add your correct answers from parts A, B, and C to get your total score. Then find the percentage for your total score on the chart below. Record your percentage on the graph on page 105.

_____ Total Score for Parts A, B, and C

_____ Percentage

Total Score	1	2	3	4	5	6	7	8	9	10	11	12	13
Percentage	8	15	23	31	38	46	54	62	69	77	85	92	100

Grant Hill

Happy to Be Back on the Court

Birth Name Grant Henry Hill

Birth Date and Place October 5, 1972; Dallas, Texas

Home Orlando, Florida

Think About What You Know

Have you, or someone you know, ever broken a bone? How long did it take for the bone to get better? Read the article and find out about Grant Hill's broken ankle.

Word Power

What do the words below tell you about the article?

rebound to catch a basketball after it bounces away from the basket

assists moves that help another player score

recovering getting better after being hurt or sick

operation something a doctor does to a person's body to help the person get well

infection what happens when germs get into a person's body and cause sickness

Reading Skill

Sequence The order of ideas in an article is called **sequence.** A good sequence clearly shows the order in which things happen. The author often uses words such as *first, next, then,* and *finally* to show the order.

Example

Happens first	Her team lost the first game. Then they won
Happens second	the next three games.

"Her team lost the first game" is the first event in the sequence. "They won the next three games" is the next event in the sequence. What words in these sentences show the sequence? What other words can you think of that might show sequence?

Grant Hill
Happy to Be Back on the Court

People called him the next Michael Jordan. That's how good he was. On the basketball court Grant Hill could do everything. He could **rebound,** dribble, pass, and shoot. But he also did the little things. He would use his body to set screens and give teammates open shots. And he played tough defense. It was no wonder that the Detroit Pistons snapped him up when he entered the NBA in 1994.

2   The Pistons were glad they did. Hill quickly became one of the best players in basketball. He was named to the All-Star team five times. In an average game, Hill scored 25 points, pulled down seven rebounds, and handed out five **assists.** Then it happened. In a playoff game in 2000, Hill broke his left ankle.

3   It was a really bad break. Doctors had to use a plate and five screws to patch up the ankle. That summer, Grant Hill became a free agent. That meant he could sign up with any team. He picked the Orlando Magic. They gave him a seven-year, $93 million deal. That was a lot of money for a player **recovering** from a broken ankle. Still, fans in Orlando were hopeful. The Magic had also signed Tracy McGrady. With those two superstars, the Magic hoped to win a championship.

4   But Hill and McGrady didn't play together long. Hill's ankle wasn't right. "I was so close and yet so far," he said later. After just four games, Hill was in too much pain to continue. So he sat out for the rest of the year. Despite that, he was named to the All-Star team for the sixth time. Hill then had a second **operation.** This time his doctors took a piece of bone from his hip. They put the bone in his ankle to give it more support.

5   This didn't work either. Something was still wrong with Hill's ankle. So doctors operated on him for the third time. In 2002 Hill played well for 29 games. But once more his ankle began to hurt. Once again Hill was done for the year.

6   In 2003 Hill had his fourth operation. This time his doctors started from scratch. First they took out the plate and all the screws. Then they cut away a piece of bone. That cut down the pressure he felt on his ankle. Finally they put in a new plate and screws. Everyone hoped that this would finally solve the problem. But there was more trouble on the way.

7   Just one week after this operation, Hill was watching TV when suddenly he felt cold. Soon he began to shake. His wife, Tamia, put blankets over him, but Hill couldn't stop shaking. Then Tamia took his temperature. It read 104 degrees. Later she checked it a second time. It read 104.5 degrees. "That's when I started to worry," she later said.

8   Tamia rushed her husband to the hospital. He was shaking so badly that nurses were forced to hold him down. "I found myself surrounded by a dozen nurses and doctors," Hill later recalled. They all looked worried.

9   Tamia began to cry. "At that point it wasn't about basketball anymore. It was about keeping him around."

Skill Break

Sequence

Look at paragraph 6 on this page. The paragraph tells about Hill's fourth operation.

What was the *first* thing the doctors did?

10   Indeed, Hill might have died. The fever was a sign that Hill had an **infection.** All the cutting and stitching had worn out the skin covering his ankle. So this time the skin had not healed properly. The cut made by the doctors had become infected. Luckily Hill began to get better. His fever slowly went down. But Hill needed a fifth operation to fix up his skin. Doctors took a chunk of skin from his left arm and used it to replace the old skin on his ankle. He missed the entire 2003–2004 season.

11   By this point, many people were wondering why Hill kept trying to go on with basketball. Why keep hoping for a comeback? Hill had already had a great, if brief, career. He had lots of money. His wife was a famous pop singer. They had a beautiful two-year-old daughter. Hill also had interests beyond basketball. He collected art and was interested in buying land. No one would have blamed him if he had hung up his basketball shoes for good.

12   But after five operations and a brush with death, Hill didn't give up. He wanted to give the sport one more try. "I'm stupid," he laughed, "or stubborn."

13   Hill's dad, Calvin, had been a star football player. So Hill knew what athletes faced when their career ended. "You don't ever get a chance to do it again," he said. "It's that old saying: An athlete dies twice. The first time is when you retire."

Fun Facts

- Hill likes to read, write, and listen to music.
- His favorite food to eat before a game is fish.
- He was 13 years old when he first dunked a basketball.
- He is 6 feet 8 inches tall.

In 2004 Grant Hill made a strong comeback to the NBA.

14   Hill worked countless hours to get ready for the 2004–2005 season. He wasn't quite the same player he had been before. But he was still very good. He averaged nearly 20 points a game. At the end of a close game, there was no one better with the ball than Hill. Even fans of other teams cheered Hill when he came on the court. "People recognize what I've been through," he said.

15   Grant Hill was so good that he was named a starter in the All-Star game. That made him happy. But most of all, Hill was happy to be back on the court. As he says, "The main thing is, I just love to play."

A Understanding What You Read

◆ **Fill in the circle next to the correct answer.**

1. Hill broke his ankle
- ○ A. during a playoff game for the Pistons.
- ○ B. while playing in a game with Tracy McGrady.
- ○ C. after signing up with the Orlando Magic.

2. What was the cause of Hill's infection?
- ○ A. His fever had reached 104.5 degrees.
- ○ B. Doctors had cut away a piece of his bone.
- ○ C. The skin on his ankle had become worn out.

3. What is one of Hill's other interests besides basketball?
- ○ A. becoming a pop singer
- ○ B. learning to cook
- ○ C. collecting art

4. In which paragraph did you find the information to answer question 3?
- ○ A. paragraph 9
- ○ B. paragraph 11
- ○ C. paragraph 13

5. What lesson about life does this story teach?
- ○ A. You learn more if you are open to new ideas.
- ○ B. Don't compare yourself to other people.
- ○ C. It's hard to give up something that you love.

_____ Number of Correct Answers: Part A

B Finding the Sequence

◆ Read the paragraph below. It shows a sequence. Number the sentences below the paragraph to show the order of what happened.

1.

Just one week after this operation, Hill was watching TV when suddenly he felt cold. Soon he began to shake. His wife, Tamia, put blankets over him, but Hill couldn't stop shaking. Then Tamia took his temperature. It read 104 degrees. Later she checked it a second time. It read 104.5 degrees. "That's when I started to worry," she later said.

_____ Tamia started to worry.

_____ Tamia put blankets over Hill.

_____ Tamia took Hill's temperature.

_____ Hill began to shake.

◆ Which words helped show you the sequence? Circle the sequence words in the paragraph. Then write the words on the lines below.

2. _____

_____

_____

_____ Number of Correct Answers: Part B

C Using Words

◆ Cross out one word in each row that does **not** fit with the word in the dark type.

1. rebound

skate   score   net   ball

2. assists

aid   tall   teamwork   help

3. recovering

sick   better   rest   sweet

4. operation

body   tomorrow   doctor   ill

5. infection

fever   medicine   ocean   germs

◆ Choose one of the words shown above in dark type. Write a sentence using the word.

6. word: _____

_____

_____

_____ Number of Correct Answers: Part C

D Writing About It

Write a Comic Strip

◆ Write a comic strip about Grant Hill. First look at what is happening in each scene. Think about what each person might be saying. Then finish the sentence in each bubble. Use the checklist on page 103 to check your work.

Lesson 5 Add your correct answers from parts A, B, and C to get your total score. Then find the percentage for your total score on the chart below. Record your percentage on the graph on page 105.

_____ Total Score for Parts A, B, and C

_____ Percentage

Total Score	1	2	3	4	5	6	7	8	9	10	11	12	13
Percentage	8	15	23	31	38	46	54	62	69	77	85	92	100

J. K. Rowling

People Love Her Stories

Birth Name Joanne Kathleen Rowling
Birth Date and Place July 31, 1965; Chipping Sodbury, England
Home Edinburgh, Scotland

Think About What You Know

Have you ever used your imagination to make up a story? What was your story about? Read the article to find out how J. K. Rowling imagined and wrote her Harry Potter story.

Word Power

What do the words below tell you about the article?

awkward not graceful

wizard a person who uses magic

carriage a small, covered bed on wheels used to carry babies

café a restaurant that serves mostly coffee

agent a person who helps writers sell their books

Reading Skill

Author's Purpose When authors write, they write for a reason. This reason is called the **author's purpose.** The author might want to tell about a person, place, or thing. The author might want to get the reader to think a certain way. The author might also want to make the reader laugh and enjoy the story.

Example

Being a writer is the best job in the world. The only tools you need are a pen, paper, and your imagination. Writers can travel anywhere they want in their stories. What other job can beat that?

In this paragraph the author's purpose is *to get the reader to think* that being a writer is a great job. One clue is that the author uses the word *best* in the first sentence. What other clues show that the author's purpose is *to get the reader to think a certain way?*

J. K. Rowling

People Love Her Stories

Are you ready for some excitement? Then step into the world of Harry Potter. Harry lives in a dangerous but magical world. It has everything from secret tunnels to evil spells. It has flying cars and talking animals. It has dragons and giants and ghosts. Harry isn't real, of course. He's a character in a book. The Harry Potter books are among the best-selling books in the world. They have sold more than 250 million copies. That has made their author, J. K. Rowling, a very well-known writer.

2   Rowling did not set out to write best sellers. She had a story in mind, and she wanted to put it down on paper. But she didn't expect it to be a big hit. She told herself that "there will be a handful of people who'll really love it." As it turned out, people all over the world love Harry.

3   Rowling grew up in England. She remembers herself as an **awkward** child. "I was shy," she says. She was short and round with "very thick" glasses. She was no good at sports. Her happiest moments came while reading or writing. "Writing is all I ever wanted to do," she says.

4   Even as a girl Rowling wrote stories. She shared them with her little sister Diane. Later she was known for telling daring tales in which she and her girlfriends played leading roles. But she rarely shared her writing with her friends.

5   When Rowling grew up, she became a secretary. But she was not very good at office work. Besides, she found it boring. "All I ever liked about working in offices was being able to type up stories on the computer when no one was looking," she says.

6   One day, while riding a train, an idea popped into Rowling's head. "I was staring out the window, and the idea for Harry just came," she says. It happened "in a flash." She imagined a boy who was a **wizard** but didn't know it. She pictured him being sent off to wizard school. "I started thinking what wizard school would be like and got so excited," she recalls. She'd had good ideas before and had written some of them down. But she had never managed to finish anything. This time, she decided, it would be different.

7   Rowling named her wizard Harry Potter. She began keeping a notebook about him. She wrote down lots of details about him and his life.

8   Meanwhile Rowling decided to change her life. In 1991, at age 26, she quit her job as a secretary and left England. She moved to Portugal and took a job teaching English. Soon she fell in love, got married, and had a baby. Although her life was busier than ever, she still found time to write about Harry.

9   Rowling's marriage did not last. In 1993 she returned to England. Now she had a problem. She had no job. She had no money. And she had a baby to support. For the next two years, Rowling barely got by. She and her daughter lived in a cold little apartment.

Skill Break

Author's Purpose

So far the author has talked about the Harry Potter books and their author, J. K. Rowling.

From what you have read so far, what might the **author's purpose** be in this article?

To get out of the apartment, Rowling often went out for walks with the baby. Rowling would put little Jessica in a baby **carriage.** Then she would head to a nearby **café.** While Jessica slept, Rowling would sit and work on her Harry Potter story. "She was quite an odd sight," recalls the café owner. He remembers her rocking the stroller back and forth with one hand and writing with the other.

10   Rowling didn't ask friends to read her story. She didn't really care what others thought of it. "I really wrote it for me," she says. She knew in her mind where she wanted the story to go. So she just kept working away at it. She says, "I spent five years writing about Harry before anyone read a single word."

11   At last, in 1995, Rowling was done. Or, at least, she was done with Harry Potter book number one. She had always known she couldn't tell the whole story in one book. She thought seven would be the right number.

12   Rowling called this first book *Harry Potter and the Philosopher's Stone.* Her **agent,** Christopher Little, sent it off to many publishers. None of them wanted it. At last, Bloomsbury Publishing showed interest. Little sold the book to Bloomsbury, and Rowling got a check for $4,000.

Fun Facts

- Rowling has a large black rabbit for a pet.
- Her Harry Potter books have been printed in over 60 languages.
- Booksellers were afraid boys would not read a book written by a woman. That's why she uses "J. K." in her name.

J. K. Rowling holds a service award she received from the Prince of Wales.

13   That was the start of big changes in Rowling's life. Her first Harry Potter book was a big success. When it was time to sell it in the United States, they changed the title to *Harry Potter and the Sorcerer's Stone.* The books that followed were even bigger hits. Hollywood began making the books into movies. And Rowling became very wealthy. By 2005 she had made over $1 billion.

14   Rowling's personal life also got brighter. In 2001 she fell in love and married again. She and her new husband had a son, David, in 2003. They had a daughter, Mackenzie, in 2005. "I am fully aware, every single day, of how lucky I am," says Rowling. Still, for all her good fortune, Rowling remains a simple person. Not long ago, she was asked what she would do if she could have any magical power. She said she would choose to be invisible. That way, she said, she could "sneak off to a café and write all day."

A Understanding What You Read

◆ **Fill in the circle next to the correct answer.**

1. The idea for Harry Potter came to Rowling while she was

○ A. teaching English classes in Portugal.
○ B. pushing her baby in a carriage.
○ C. looking out the window on a train.

2. Rowling didn't share her Harry Potter story with anyone for five years because she

○ A. was writing the story for herself.
○ B. wanted to check it for mistakes first.
○ C. couldn't find anyone who would read it.

3. From what you read in the article, which of these is probably true?

○ A. Being a secretary made Rowling a better writer.
○ B. Rowling's writing helped her get through hard times.
○ C. Rowling's friends knew that she would become a writer.

4. Choose the statement below that states an opinion.

○ A. Rowling grew up in England.
○ B. Rowling became a secretary.
○ C. Rowling remains a simple person.

5. From the information in the article, you can predict that Rowling will

○ A. soon move to Hollywood.
○ B. sell more books to Bloomsbury.
○ C. become a writing teacher.

_____ Number of Correct Answers: Part A

B Finding the Author's Purpose

◆ What is the author's purpose for writing the article about J. K. Rowling? Fill in the circle next to the answer that **best** states the author's purpose.

1.

○ A. to tell the reader about a famous author
○ B. to get the reader to go see a Harry Potter movie
○ C. to make the reader laugh at Rowling's jokes

◆ Read the short article below. What is the author's purpose for writing the article? Fill in the circle next to the answer that **best** states the author's purpose.

2.

My friend Ernie can't get enough of J. K. Rowling's books. Ernie has read every Harry Potter book at least three times. He reads on the bus. He reads at the dinner table. He even reads in the bathtub! One time he came to school without shoes. He was so caught up in his reading that he didn't even notice!

Last week Ernie started to talk in a Harry Potter voice. He dresses like him too. To be more like Harry, Ernie drew a "Z" on his forehead with his mom's lipstick. His parents are starting to worry.

○ A. to tell the reader about Ernie's new books
○ B. to get the reader to read more Harry Potter books
○ C. to make the reader laugh about what Ernie does

_____ Number of Correct Answers: Part B

C Using Words

◆ Cross out one word in each row that does **not** fit with the word in the dark type.

1. awkward

cold   shy   difficult   stiff

2. wizard

wand   spell   cowboy   magic

3. carriage

roll   baby   wheels   jewels

4. café

buy   sit   run   drink

5. agent

book   laughing   writer   printing

◆ Choose one of the words shown above in dark type. Write a sentence using the word.

6. word: _____

_____

_____

```
┌─────────────────────────────────────────┐
│  _____ Number of Correct Answers: Part C │
└─────────────────────────────────────────┘
```

 **Writing About It**

Write a Story

◆ What happened when J. K. Rowling heard that her first book had been sold? Write a story about that day. Finish the sentences below to write your story. Use the checklist on page 103 to check your work.

One day J. K. Rowling got a call from Christopher Little. He told

her that _____

_____.

When Rowling heard the news, she felt _____.

She remembered when _____

_____.

Rowling didn't expect _____.

She had no idea how many people would read her book.

Lesson 6 Add your correct answers from parts A, B, and C to get your total score. Then find the percentage for your total score on the chart below. Record your percentage on the graph on page 105.

_____ Total Score for Parts A, B, and C

_____ Percentage

Total Score	1	2	3	4	5	6	7	8	9	10	11	12	13
Percentage	8	15	23	31	38	46	54	62	69	77	85	92	100

Compare and Contrast

◆ Think about the celebrities, or famous people, in Unit Two. Pick two articles that tell about celebrities who showed talent when they were young. Use information from the articles to fill in this chart.

Celebrity's Name		
What was the first sign that the celebrity had talent?		
How did the celebrity grow his or her talent?		
Where did the celebrity's talent lead?		

Dale Earnhardt Jr.

Alicia Keys

Michelle Kwan

Dale Earnhardt Jr.

A Son to Be Proud Of

Birth Name Ralph Dale Earnhardt Jr.

Birth Date and Place October 10, 1974; Kannapolis, North Carolina

Home Mooresville, North Carolina

Think About What You Know

Is there someone in your life that you admire? Would you like to learn from that person? Read the article to find out how Dale Earnhardt Jr. learned from his father.

Word Power

What do the words below tell you about the article?

guidance the giving of help and direction

ranks levels of experience and position

division a part or section

tributes speeches and other ceremonies held to honor someone

compliment a type of praise

Reading Skill

Main Idea and Supporting Details The **main idea** gives a paragraph its purpose and direction. The paragraph's **details** support and explain the main idea. There may be many details in a paragraph but only one main idea. The supporting details are specific ideas. The main idea is a more general idea.

Example	
Main Idea	Car racing is a dangerous sport. Race cars can go more than 200 miles an hour. Drivers can be hurt or
Supporting Details	killed in high-speed crashes. Safety gear, such as helmets, harnesses, and fireproof suits, is very important.

"Car racing is a dangerous sport" is the main idea. What are the supporting details?

Dale Earnhardt Jr.

A Son to Be Proud Of

There was just one person in the world Dale Earnhardt Jr. trusted completely. There was one person he looked to for support and **guidance.** That person was his father, Dale Earnhardt. But on February 18, 2001, Earnhardt Sr. died. He was killed in a car crash at the Daytona 500. That left a big question. What would Earnhardt Jr. do now? Would he continue to race in the very sport that killed his father?

2   Earnhardt Jr. grew up in the shadow of his father. Almost everyone called him "Junior" or "Little E." His father was, of course, the "Big E." By the time Earnhardt Jr. was a teenager, Big E had already won three Winston Cup championships. The elder Earnhardt went on to win four more. He made millions of dollars. He became one of the most famous drivers in the world. As one writer put it, Earnhardt Sr. was "the heart and soul" of NASCAR racing.

3   Earnhardt Jr. was proud of his father. And he wanted his father to be proud of him. He wanted to prove that he, too, could be a world-class driver. Having a famous father didn't make it any easier for Earnhardt Jr. He started at the beginning, just like everybody else. He once said, "I got started in racing by getting up $500 and buying a street car out of the junkyard, building it into a street stock car when I was 17 years old."

4   Over the next few years, Earnhardt Jr. worked his way up through the **ranks.** He struggled at first. But soon he started winning race after race. During this time, he studied his father's style carefully. As one man said, Earnhardt Jr. "watched every move his dad made and stored it for when the time would come when he'd need to do it."

5   In 2000 25-year-old Earnhardt Jr. made it into the top NASCAR **division.** For the first time, he would be in the same Winston Cup races as his father. He knew that racing fans would be watching him. They would all be comparing him to his father. Earnhardt Jr. didn't want to disappoint them. More importantly, he didn't want to disappoint his father. He wanted to show that he was deserving enough to be called an Earnhardt.

6   It didn't take Earnhardt Jr. long to prove himself. In April 2000, in Fort Worth, Texas, he got his first Winston Cup win. Most drivers compete in dozens of races before winning their first Winston Cup. Earnhardt Jr. did it in his twelfth start. He took the lead in lap 282 and held it for the remaining 53 laps. He crossed the finish line six full seconds ahead of the second-place driver.

7   After his victory lap, Dale Jr. rolled to a stop. His father, who had finished seventh, rushed over to him. Earnhardt Sr. stuck his head into his son's car. "He just told me he loved me," Dale Jr. said later. "He wanted to make sure I took the time to enjoy this."

8   Dale Jr. was thrilled. He had shown that he could compete with the best drivers in the world. He thought that he and his father could look forward to years of racing together. But less than a year later, tragedy struck. On the last lap of the Daytona 500, Earnhardt Sr.'s car spun out of control. He crashed into a wall and was killed instantly.

Skill Break
Main Idea and Supporting Details
Look at paragraph 6 on this page. The paragraph tells about one of Earnhardt Jr.'s important races.

What is the **main idea** of the paragraph?

What **details** support the main idea?

9   No one could believe it. All around the country, people mourned. One newspaper called it "Daytona's Darkest Day." Another called it simply "Black Sunday."

10   Earnhardt Jr. felt more shock and pain than any fan. The man he loved most in the world was gone. Earnhardt Jr. was on the race track when it happened. He crossed the finish line in second place just as his father crashed. Some people wondered if that would be the last race Earnhardt Jr. ever entered. They wondered if he might leave the sport that killed his father. But Earnhardt Jr. knew what his father would have wanted. "We'll get through this," he told one radio station. "I'm sure he'd want us to keep going, and that's what we're going to do."

11   And so, just one week after his father's death, Earnhardt Jr. returned to racing. It wasn't easy. Everywhere he went, race tracks held special **tributes** to his father. At every stop, fans asked him to sign his father's picture.

12   One of the toughest moments came in July 2001 at the Pepsi 400. That's when Dale Jr. returned to Daytona for the first time since Earnhardt Sr.'s death. Dale Jr. went out that day with fire in his eyes. He wanted to honor his father's memory by racing better than ever. And he did. Dale Jr. blew past the other cars and won the race. Then he picked up his radio. He said to his crew, "Y'all know who that's for, guys."

Fun Facts

▶ Earnhardt Jr. likes playing computer games.

▶ The book he wrote, *Driver #8*, was a best seller for 17 weeks.

▶ He has a dance floor in his basement that's big enough for 225 people.

Dale Earnhardt Jr. celebrates a victory with his stepmother Teresa Earnhardt.

13 Less than three years later, Earnhardt Jr. won the most important victory of all. He took first place in the Daytona 500, the same race that had killed his father. "This is the greatest day of my life," Earnhardt Jr. said after the race. He admitted that he had been thinking about his father as he made the final laps. "I felt like he was in the passenger seat with me today," Earnhardt Jr. said. "I know he's smiling right now."

14 Earnhardt Jr. now stood on his own as one of NASCAR's best racers. Still, neither he nor the fans would ever forget Dale Earnhardt Sr. Said Dale Jr., "The biggest **compliment** you can give me is that I remind you of my dad."

A Understanding What You Read

◆ Fill in the circle next to the correct answer.

1. When Dale Jr. was 17 years old, he

○ A. bought a street car from the junkyard.
○ B. made it to the top NASCAR division.
○ C. won the Daytona 500.

2. From what you read in this article, Dale Jr. and Earnhardt Sr. are different because

○ A. only Earnhardt Sr. grew up with a famous father.
○ B. Earnhardt Sr. won the Winston Cup but Dale Jr. never did.
○ C. only Dale Jr. learned to win races by watching his father.

3. What did Earnhardt Sr. do after Dale Jr. won his first Winston Cup?

○ A. He got in the passenger seat.
○ B. He told Dale Jr. that he loved him.
○ C. He asked Dale Jr. to be more careful.

4. If you were a beginning race car driver, how might you use the information in the article to improve your driving?

○ A. I would find drivers that I admired and learn from them.
○ B. I would study carefully the history of NASCAR racing.
○ C. I would ask someone in my family to help me buy a race car.

5. The author probably wrote this article in order to

○ A. keep the reader from wanting to race cars.
○ B. make the reader laugh at amusing racing stories.
○ C. tell the reader about a famous father-son relationship.

_____ Number of Correct Answers: Part A

B Finding the Main Idea and Supporting Details

◆ Read the paragraph below. Fill in the circle next to the sentence that is the **best** main idea for the paragraph.

1.

One of the toughest moments came in July 2001 at the Pepsi 400. That's when Dale Jr. returned to Daytona for the first time since Earnhardt Sr.'s death. Dale Jr. went out that day with fire in his eyes. He wanted to honor his father's memory by racing better than ever. And he did. Dale Jr. blew past the other cars and won the race. Then he picked up his radio. He said to his crew, "Y'all know who that's for, guys."

○ A. Dale Jr. blew past the other cars and won the race.
○ B. He wanted to honor his father's memory by racing better than ever.
○ C. One of the toughest moments came in July 2001 at the Pepsi 400.

◆ Read the paragraph below. Write the main idea of the paragraph and one supporting detail.

2.

Less than three years later, Earnhardt Jr. won the most important victory of all. He took first place in the Daytona 500, the same race that had killed his father. "This is the greatest day of my life," Earnhardt Jr. said after the race. He admitted that he had been thinking about his father as he made the final laps. "I felt like he was in the passenger seat with me today," Earnhardt Jr. said. "I know he's smiling right now."

Main Idea: _____

Supporting Detail: _____

_____ Number of Correct Answers: Part B

C Using Words

◆ The words or phrases in the list below relate to the words in the box. Some words or phrases in the list have a meaning that is the same as or similar to a word in the box. Some words have the opposite meaning. Write the related word from the box on each line. Use each word from the box twice.

guidance	division	compliment
ranks	tributes	

Same or similar meaning

1. levels _____

2. advice _____

3. grades _____

4. honoring events _____

5. part _____

6. flattery _____

7. ceremonies _____

8. teaching _____

Opposite meaning

9. insult _____

10. whole _____

_____ Number of Correct Answers: Part C

74

D Writing About It

Write a Description

◆ Write a description of what happened in 2001 and 2004 at the Daytona 500. Finish the sentences below to write your description. Use the checklist on page 103 to check your work.

The Daytona 500 is one of the biggest NASCAR races. February 18, 2001, was called "Daytona's Darkest Day." On that day, _____

_____ .

His son, Dale Jr., was _____

_____ .

Three years later, at the 2004 Daytona 500, _____

_____ .

The Earnhardt name has become a legend in Daytona 500 history.

Lesson 7 Add your correct answers from parts A, B, and C to get your total score. Then find the percentage for your total score on the chart below. Record your percentage on the graph on page 105.

_____ Total Score for Parts A, B, and C

_____ Percentage

Total Score	1	2	3	4	5	6	7	8	9	10	11	12	13	14	15	16	17
Percentage	6	12	18	24	29	35	41	47	53	59	65	71	76	82	88	94	100

Alicia Keys
Music from the Heart

Birth Name Alicia Augello Cook
Birth Date and Place January 25, 1981; Manhattan, New York
Home New York City

Think About What You Know

Have you ever wanted to express your own style? Did you feel free to be yourself? Read the article to find out about Alicia Keys and her style of music.

Word Power

What do the words below tell you about the article?

survivor someone who has lived through hard times

genius an unusual and special talent

credit praise for work done or help given

scholarship an award that pays for school

referred was related

Reading Skill

Sequence The order of ideas in an article is called **sequence.** A good sequence clearly shows the order in which things happen. The author often uses words such as *first, next, then,* and *finally* to show the order.

Example	
Happens first	First Jane wrote new songs of her own. Then
Happens second	she practiced and recorded each song. Several
Happens third	months later, she finally finished her record.

The sequence above shows the order of three events. What words in the paragraph help show the order?

Alicia Keys

Music from the Heart

Alicia Keys is a **survivor.** She is also a music superstar. Her albums have sold in the millions. She sang at the Super Bowl in 2005. She has won many major music awards. Her first album, *Songs in A Minor,* won five Grammies. And her career is just beginning. There is no telling how far she might go. But her life wasn't always so grand.

2   She was born Alicia Augello Cook in 1981. Her father, Craig Cook, left the family two years later. Her mother, Terri Augello, had to raise Alicia alone. But Terri wasn't home much. She had to work two jobs in order to get money to buy food and pay the rent. She worked all day and at night. Says Alicia, "I don't know how she stood up from day to day."

3   Keys and her mother lived in a tough part of New York City called Hell's Kitchen. "It was kind of a cool spot," Keys says, "but 42nd Street then was no heaven." There was danger around every corner, especially at night. In fact, Keys was attacked at least once. Keys doesn't like to talk much about those times. She does say that she fought back but was never seriously hurt.

4   At school Keys didn't fit in with other kids. "I didn't have the same thoughts in my head as the other kids in school," she once said. "It was lonely, but I never felt alone because I always had my mother."

5   Keys grew up fast. Even as a child, she made many of her own decisions. "I spent most of my time on my own," she says. "I had nobody standing behind me, telling me what to do. I had to figure everything out for myself." By the time she was 11, she thought of herself as an adult. "I'd given up playing with dolls years earlier. My mother and I were like equals."

6   Keys had something else going for her: talent. Lots of kids can sing or play the piano at an early age, but Keys was different. Her talent was more like musical **genius.** She began to sing as soon as she learned to talk. Seeing Alicia's talent, Terri struggled to save money for piano lessons. Then a family friend gave them an old piano. It took up a lot of space in their tiny apartment. "It ended up being the divider between the living room and my bedroom," recalls Keys.

7   Keys began to study classical piano. She played the music of Mozart and Chopin. She also studied jazz. And she learned from the music she heard outside her window. Neighbors gathered on street corners and made hip-hop music. Keys learned to rap. "That's one of my fondest memories—of all these people coming together and having a good time," she says. "It was all very free, with nobody saying what you should or shouldn't do when it came to music."

Fun Facts

- Keys likes to watch movies and go swimming.
- She first performed on stage when she was four years old.
- Before she changed her name to Keys, she thought about calling herself Alicia Wild.

8   As a teenager, Keys began writing her own songs. She went to high school at the Professional Performing Arts School. At nights she sang and played piano as part of a four-girl singing group. Mostly they sang in Harlem. She often gives **credit** for her musical training to "the Two H's": Harlem and Hell's Kitchen.

9   Keys was an "A" student. In 1996 she graduated from high school first in her class. Then she had to make a tough choice. Columbia University offered her a **scholarship.** She also had a contract with Columbia Records. Keys chose college. But then she left after a few weeks. Her love of music was simply too great. She wanted to develop her singing career.

10   Things at the record company did not go well. The people there tried to make her into something she wasn't. "I hated it," she says. "I remember driving to the studio one day feeling dread in my chest."

11   At last Keys left Columbia Records. She then signed with Arista. The head of this record label was Clive Davis. He had discovered huge stars such as Janis Joplin and Whitney Houston. Davis asked Keys a simple question. He asked her who she wanted to be.

12   After signing her, Davis let Keys create her own style of music. That style is free to change. Keys refuses to give it a label. "I want to float wherever my heart goes," she told TV host Oprah Winfrey. "My music is heart music. Giving it any other description is dangerous."

Skill Break

Sequence

Look at paragraph 9 on this page. The paragraph tells about the beginning of Keys's singing career.

What *two* things did Keys do after she graduated from high school?

On a day when she has a show, Keys does not talk at all until around 6 P.M.

13   Davis himself left Arista in 1999. Then he set up a new label called J Records and took Alicia with him.

14   Alicia had changed her last name to Keys. She liked the name because it **referred** to the keys on a piano. It also pointed to the unlocking of doors. It reminded Alicia that there are "things as yet unknown to myself that I plan to open."

15   Keys's first album went straight to the top of the charts in 2001. *Songs in A Minor* sold ten million copies. Some people thought her success came quickly. In a sense it did. But Alicia Keys didn't wake up one morning a star. She has worked toward this goal all her life. As she puts it, "People think you're an overnight success because this is the first time they've seen you. It's just that no one ever sees you when you're heads-down and working hard in the shadows."

A Understanding What You Read

◆ Fill in the circle next to the correct answer.

1. Why was Keys's mother away from home a lot?

○ A. She was in a singing group.
○ B. She was looking for a piano.
○ C. She had to work two jobs.

2. Choose the statement below that states a fact.

○ A. Alicia Keys writes the most beautiful songs.
○ B. Alicia Keys sang at the Super Bowl in 2005.
○ C. Alicia Keys found success too quickly.

3. Why did Keys leave Columbia Records?

○ A. She wanted to be free with her music.
○ B. She wanted to stay at home with her mother.
○ C. She wanted to go to college to study jazz.

4. In which paragraph did you find the information to answer question 3?

○ A. paragraph 8
○ B. paragraph 10
○ C. paragraph 12

5. Which sentence **best** states the main idea of the article?

○ A. Alicia Keys got musical training while growing up in Harlem.
○ B. Alicia Keys knows the right people to work with in music.
○ C. Alicia Keys has found success while staying true to herself.

_____ Number of Correct Answers: Part A

B Finding the Sequence

◆ Read the paragraphs below. They show a sequence. Write what happened first, second, and third.

1.

　. At last Keys left Columbia Records. She then signed with Arista. The head of this record label was Clive Davis. He had discovered huge stars such as Janis Joplin and Whitney Houston. Davis asked Keys a simple question. He asked her who she wanted to be.

　After signing her, Davis let Keys create her own style of music. That style is free to change. Keys refuses to give it a label. "I want to float wherever my heart goes," she told TV host Oprah Winfrey. "My music is heart music. Giving it any other description is dangerous."

First: _____

Second: _____

Third: _____

◆ Which words helped show you the sequence? Circle the sequence words in the paragraphs. Then write the words on the lines below.

2. _____

_____

_____

_____ Number of Correct Answers: Part B

C Using Words

◆ Complete each sentence with a word from the box. Write the missing word on the line.

survivor	credit	referred
genius	scholarship	

1. He is going to try to get a _____ to a good college.

2. I give my parents _____ for teaching me to be

kind to others.

3. Her very first painting showed signs of _____.

4. After the forest fire, the only _____ was a small

oak tree.

5. The book's title _____ to the author's home town.

◆ Choose one word from the box. Write a new sentence using the word.

6. word: _____

_____

_____ Number of Correct Answers: Part C

D Writing About It

Write an Advertisement

◆ Write an advertisement for an Alicia Keys concert. Finish the sentences below to write your advertisement. Use the checklist on page 103 to check your work.

See Alicia Keys Live in Concert!

This Saturday Alicia Keys is coming to town for a live concert.

At the concert you will hear _____

_____ .

Keys is a great performer. She has won many music awards,

including _____ .

Her musical training comes from _____

_____ .

Lesson 8 Add your correct answers from parts A, B, and C to get your total score. Then find the percentage for your total score on the chart below. Record your percentage on the graph on page 105.

_____ Total Score for Parts A, B, and C

_____ Percentage

Total Score	1	2	3	4	5	6	7	8	9	10	11	12	13
Percentage	8	15	23	31	38	46	54	62	69	77	85	92	100

Michelle Kwan

She Certainly Loves to Skate

Birth Name Michelle Wing Kwan

Birth Date and Place July 7, 1980; Torrance, California

Home Los Angeles, California

Think About What You Know

Have you ever come very close to winning but then lost instead? What did that feel like? Read the article to find out how Michelle Kwan learned to accept both winning and losing.

Word Power

What do the words below tell you about the article?

underdog the one who is most likely to lose

competitions contests

overwhelmed made helpless

choreographer someone who creates dance moves

disagreement a difference of opinion

Reading Skill

Author's Purpose The reason an author writes is called the **author's purpose.** The author might want to tell about a person, place, or thing. The author might want to make the reader think a certain way. The author might also want to entertain the reader.

Example

Two types of jumps in figure skating are toe jumps and edge jumps. In a toe jump, the skater pushes off the ice with the front point of one skate. In an edge jump, the skater uses the edge of a skate blade to push off the ice.

In this paragraph, the author's purpose is *to tell about* two types of skating jumps. One clue is that the author gives facts to help the reader learn something. What other clues show that the author's purpose is *to tell about* something?

Michelle Kwan

She Certainly Loves to Skate

Michelle Kwan has been called lots of names. She has been called everything from a tiger to a swan. One expert says she is "the greatest skater in the world." Another says she is "too slow." One says she's a "genius." Another says she is "crazy." As Kwan herself puts it, "I've been the favorite. I've been the **underdog.** I've been the 'little jumping bean.' I've been everything."

2   So who *is* Michelle Kwan really? She may be a mixture of all these things. But whatever else she is, one thing is certain. She's a young woman who loves to skate.

3   Kwan put on her first pair of ice skates in 1985, when she was just five years old. Her older brother was playing hockey at a rink near their home in Torrance, California. Kwan and her seven-year-old sister, Karen, wanted to get on the ice, too, so their parents signed them up for figure skating lessons. Both girls showed promise, but from the beginning Michelle's talent stood out. She was very natural on the ice. "To her it was like walking," says Karen.

4   Kwan began spending all her free time skating. She would get up very early in the morning and hurry to the rink. She even slept in her skating costume so she wouldn't have to waste time getting dressed. She skated from 5 A.M. to 8 A.M. every weekday and then went to school. On weekends her parents drove her two hours to a special training rink for more skating. "Every weekend she'd learn a new jump," recalls Karen.

5   Most skaters take at least eight years to work their way up through the different levels of skating. Kwan did it in less than five. During that time, she skated every day, no matter what. She skated when she had a cold and when she was tired. She skated when she had the flu. She even skated when she had chicken pox.

6   Kwan's efforts paid off. In 1994, when she was just 13 years old, she finished second at the U.S. Championships. She came in eighth at the World Championships. Two years later, she won both **competitions.** Kwan then went on to win more awards than any female skater in U.S. history. By 2005 she had won nine U.S. titles and five world titles. She has been without question the most successful skater of her time.

7   Why, then, do people have such mixed impressions of her? It may have something to do with the 1998 and 2002 Olympic Games. Going into the 1998 Olympics, Kwan was the favorite. Everyone thought she would win the gold medal. But she didn't. The pressure seemed to get to her. She did not skate with her usual grace and style. Reporters said she seemed "cautious" and "careful." Even her coach, Frank Carroll, said that Kwan looked unsure of herself. "I was **overwhelmed,**" Kwan later said. "I didn't want to make a mistake."

Skill Break
Author's Purpose
So far the author has talked about Michelle Kwan and her skating career. From what you have read so far, what might the **author's purpose** be in this article?

8   Meanwhile Kwan's teammate Tara Lipinski leaped around the ice with joy and enthusiasm. In the end it was Lipinski, not Kwan, who won the gold medal. Kwan had to settle for silver. She later called this "the hardest moment of my life." She had come so close to winning and had seen it slip away.

9   Kwan bounced back, however. Over the next three years she won more than a dozen major championships. Again and again she dazzled judges and fans with her grace and skill. In 2002 she again made the Olympic team. But once again things went wrong. This time the trouble started long before Kwan got to the Olympic village. Eight months before the competition, Kwan fired her **choreographer,** Lori Nichols. For eight years Nichols had helped Kwan put her moves together. Now Kwan said she didn't need Nichols's help anymore. Kwan's next choice was even more surprising. She fired Frank Carroll, her coach of nine years.

10   "I was shocked," Carroll said. "If there had been some argument, some **disagreement,** about her skating, I'd maybe understand. But there wasn't anything like that."

11   Kwan didn't feel the need to explain. When reporters asked her why she had fired Carroll, she said simply, "I need to be strong. I need to stand on my own two feet."

Fun Facts

▶ Kwan had a pet squirrel when she was young.

▶ Her nickname is Shelly.

▶ She always wears a good-luck necklace that her grandmother gave her.

Michelle Kwan performs in Salt Lake City during the 2002 Olympic Games.

12   So heading into the Olympics, Kwan had no coach at all. People didn't know what to think. Some hoped she could win gold all by herself. Others thought she had lost her mind even to try.

13   Early in the competition, it looked as though Kwan could win. But once again she failed to do so. In her final performance, she missed one of her moves and almost came to a complete stop. A younger teammate, Sarah Hughes, beat her. So did a Russian skater. Kwan came in third.

14   Despite the Olympic losses, Kwan remains one of the biggest names in figure skating. She has had one of the longest careers in the history of the sport. And she is still skating. As Kwan sees it, there is no reason to stop. "I still enjoy it," she says. "I'm the luckiest girl alive that I get to perform in front of thousands of people, doing what I love."

15   And she *does* love it. "When I'm on the ice, I think of the pure joy of skating," she says. "I'm skating for the love of it, for the fun."

A Understanding What You Read

◆ Fill in the circle next to the correct answer.

1. From what you read in paragraphs 4 and 5, which of these is probably true?

○ A. Kwan often got sick from too much skating.
○ B. Kwan was determined to become a great skater.
○ C. Kwan spent most of her free time with school friends.

2. What happened when Kwan was 13 years old?

○ A. She finished second at the U.S. Championships.
○ B. She decided to fire her choreographer, Lori Nichols.
○ C. She won a silver medal at the Olympic Games.

3. Why wasn't Kwan able to skate as well as she could have in the 1998 Olympics?

○ A. At the last moment she tried to change her skating style.
○ B. She had a disagreement with her coach, Frank Carroll.
○ C. The pressure to do well was too much for her.

4. From the information in the article, you can predict that Kwan will

○ A. choose to keep skating for as long as she can.
○ B. continue to be a cautious, careful skater.
○ C. hire her old coach and choreographer again.

5. Which of the following groups would this article fit into?

○ A. Great but Unknown Skaters
○ B. Lives of World Champion Skaters
○ C. Short Careers in Skating

_____ Number of Correct Answers: Part A

B Finding the Author's Purpose

◆ What is the author's purpose for writing the article about Michelle Kwan? Fill in the circle next to the answer that **best** states the author's purpose.

1.

○ A. to get the reader to want to learn to ice skate
○ B. to tell the reader about a famous ice skater
○ C. to make the reader laugh about a funny skating story

◆ Read the short article below. What is the author's purpose for writing the article? Fill in the circle next to the answer that **best** states the author's purpose.

2.

Michelle Kwan is definitely the best figure skater the world has ever seen. Not only does she have great skating talent, but she also has grace and style. She can affect people's feelings as she skates. People often begin to cry as they watch her float over the ice.

Kwan has proved her skill in competitions. She holds the record for medals won at the World Championships. She has won a total of eight medals: five gold and three silver. No one in history has won more than that. In addition, she won her first World Championship when she was only 15 years old. One coach has even called her "a genius of skating."

○ A. to tell the reader about Kwan's grace and style
○ B. to make the reader laugh about Kwan's unusual coach
○ C. to get the reader to think that Kwan is a great skater

_____ Number of Correct Answers: Part B

C Using Words

◆ The words and phrases in the list below relate to the words in the box. Some words or phrases in the list have a meaning that is the same as or similar to a word in the box. Some have the opposite meaning. Write the related word from the box on each line. Use each word from the box twice.

underdog	overwhelmed	disagreement
competitions	choreographer	

Same or similar meaning

1. quarrel _____

2. dance creator _____

3. the least favored _____

4. races with a winner _____

5. artist _____

6. can't take anymore _____

Opposite meaning

7. feeling confident _____

8. games just for fun _____

9. same opinion _____

10. champion _____

_____ Number of Correct Answers: Part C

94

D Writing About It

Write a Journal Entry

◆ Suppose you had seen Michelle Kwan skate at the 2002 Olympic Games. Write a journal entry about what you saw. Finish the sentences below to write your journal entry. Use the checklist on page 103 to check your work.

Yesterday I saw Michelle Kwan skate in the Olympic Games. I wanted to see her skate because _____

_____.

Since she did not win a gold medal in 1998, I thought that _____

_____.

It was too bad when _____.

I think Michelle Kwan _____

_____.

Lesson 9 Add your correct answers from parts A, B, and C to get your total score. Then find the percentage for your total score on the chart below. Record your percentage on the graph on page 105.

_____ Total Score for Parts A, B, and C

_____ Percentage

Total Score	1	2	3	4	5	6	7	8	9	10	11	12	13	14	15	16	17
Percentage	6	12	18	24	29	35	41	47	53	59	65	71	76	82	88	94	100

Compare and Contrast

◆ Think about the celebrities, or famous people, in Unit Three. Pick two articles that tell about celebrities who experienced big losses. Use information from the articles to fill in this chart.

Celebrity's Name		
What was the celebrity's loss?		
How did the loss happen?		
How did the celebrity get over the loss?		

Glossary

A

agent   a person who helps writers sell their books   p. 58

assists   moves that help another player score   p. 46

audition   to try out for a part in a play or movie   p. 37

awkward   not graceful   p. 56

C

café   a restaurant that serves mostly coffee   p. 58

canopy   a tentlike covering that blocks the sun   p. 6

career   the type of work someone chooses to do   p. 5

carriage   a small, covered bed on wheels used to carry babies   p. 58

choreographer   someone who creates dance moves   p. 90

communicating   sharing ideas and feelings   p. 37

companies   groups of people who make or sell something   p. 26

competitions   contests   p. 89

compliment   a type of praise   p. 71

confident   sure of one's self   p. 5

credit   praise for work done or help given   p. 80

D

desperate   having little or no hope   p. 16

disagreement   a difference of opinion   p. 90

disaster   a terrible event   p. 16

division   a part or section   p. 69

drills   practice that is the same each time   p. 24

G

gallery   a place where art is sold   p. 17

genius   an unusual and special talent   p. 79

guidance   the giving of help and direction   p. 68

I

infection   what happens when germs get into a person's body
and cause sickness   p. 48

intelligent   able to think and learn   p. 4

J

jockey   a person who rides a race horse   p. 39

L

local   within the same town   p. 14

O

operation   something a doctor does to a person's body to help the person get well   p. 46

overwhelmed   made helpless   p. 89

P

physical   having to do with the body   p. 38

producer   a person in charge of making a work of art   p. 15

R

ranks   levels of experience and position   p. 68

rebound   to catch a basketball after it bounces away from the basket   p. 46

recovering   getting better after being hurt or sick   p. 46

referred   was related   p. 81

S

scholarship   an award that pays for school   p. 80

skinny   very thin   p. 25

sprained   hurt by bending too far   p. 26

stretcher   a small bed used to carry someone who is hurt   p. 26

strict   keeping tight control   p. 4

stunts   dangerous actions   p. 39

survivor   someone who has lived through hard times   p. 78

T

tributes   speeches and other ceremonies held to honor someone   p. 70

U

underdog   the one who is most likely to lose   p. 88

W

wizard   a person who uses magic   p. 57

My Personal Dictionary

My Personal Dictionary

Writing Checklist

1. I followed the directions for writing.

2. My writing shows that I read and understood the article.

3. I capitalized the names of people.

4. I capitalized the proper names of places and things.

5. I read my writing aloud and listened for missing words.

6. I used a dictionary to check words that don't look right.

◆ Use the chart below to check off the things on the list that you have done.

✔	Lesson Numbers								
Checklist Numbers	**1**	**2**	**3**	**4**	**5**	**6**	**7**	**8**	**9**
1.									
2.									
3.									
4.									
5.									
6.									

Progress Check

You can take charge of your own progress. The Comprehension and Critical Thinking Progress Graph on the next page can help you. Use it to keep track of how you are doing as you work through the lessons in this book. Check the graph often with your teacher. What types of skills cause you trouble? Talk with your teacher about ways to work on these.

A sample Comprehension and Critical Thinking Progress Graph is shown below. The first three lessons have been filled in to show you how to use the graph.

Sample Comprehension and Critical Thinking Progress Graph

◆ **Directions:** Write your percentage score for each lesson in the box under the number of the lesson. Then put a small X on the line. The X goes above the number of the lesson and across from the score you earned. Chart your progress by drawing a line to connect the Xs.

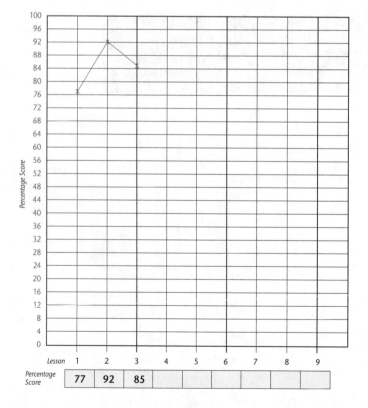

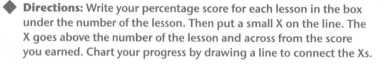

Comprehension and Critical Thinking Progress Graph

◆ **Directions:** Write your percentage score for each lesson in the box under the number of the lesson. Then put a small X on the line. The X goes above the number of the lesson and across from the score you earned. Chart your progress by drawing a line to connect the Xs.

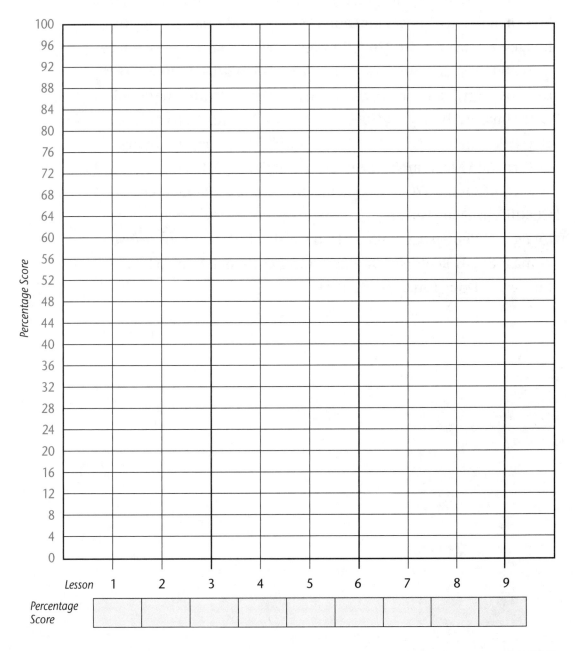

Photo Credits